A small and passionate team works behind the scenes on **Fresh**. Through our wonderful presenters we are committed to inspiring our viewers and readers to cook because we believe good food makes you happy.

This is **Fresh's** first book. The recipes have been hand-picked by the team from a list of personal favourites.

They deserve to step out of the shadows for making **Fresh** the gem that it is. Thankyou.

Robyn Wade
Executive Producer
Fresh

Supervising Production Chef	Michelle Lucia
Production Chef	Rob Cowan
Production Chef	Naomi Smith
Production Manager	Lisa Guthridge
Senior Producer	Shani Hatton
Producer	Kate Pulsford
Producer	Naomi Rechter
Producer	Andy Carmichael
Assistant Producer	Rebecca Pullman
Producton Assistant	Harriet Burton Taylor

Front cover - Spanish potato salad, see page 13 for recipe

Back cover - chocolate, hazelnut stack, see page 67 for recipe

Photography by Christian Mushenko

ISBN 978-0-646-49309-1

First published in Australia in 2008 by Nine Network Australia Pty Limited

PO Box 27 Willoughby NSW 2068 Australia

contents

chestnut & spinach soup

serves 6-8

500g fresh chestnuts
30g butter
2 leeks, white part only, sliced thinly
2 parsnips, peeled and diced
1 bunch English spinach, washed well and chopped
6 cups chicken stock
salt and pepper
200ml crème fraiche or sour cream

toasted sourdough bread to serve

Place chestnuts in a large saucepan and cover with cold water. Bring to the boil, remove from heat, take out one chestnut at a time and strip off both outer and inner skin with a sharp knife. Reserve chestnut 'meat' and set aside.

Heat butter in a large pan over medium heat and cook leeks, stirring frequently until collapsed but not coloured.

Add parsnips and chestnuts and continue cooking for a further 5 minutes, or until parsnips have softened. Stir in spinach and stock. Season with salt and pepper.

Bring to the boil; reduce heat and simmer 20 minutes or until vegetables are cooked.

Puree until smooth and return to the heat; stir through crème fraiche. Divide soup into large heated bowls. Season with freshly ground black pepper and serve with toasted sourdough bread.

fresh
NINE NETWORK

The easiest way to eat chestnuts is to roast, grill or barbecue them. Make a small cut in the shell before cooking.

chicken laksa

2 x 100g vermicelli rice noodles
150g bean shoots
12 fried tofu puffs, halved
2 small chicken breast fillets, steamed
2 tablespoons vegetable oil
¼ cup laksa paste
800ml chicken stock
400ml can coconut milk
1 tablespoon sugar
pinch salt to taste
2-3 kaffir lime leaves, finely shredded

fresh coriander sprigs and lime wedges to serve

Place noodles into a large heat proof bowl and pour enough boiling water to cover. Stand 5 minutes or until softened; drain and divide amongst four large soup bowls. Add half of the bean shoots and fried tofu; reserve the rest for garnish.

Slice cooked chicken breasts into thin slices and set aside.

Heat oil in a pan over medium heat and add laksa paste. Cook, stirring for a few minutes or until paste is fragrant. Stir in stock, coconut milk and sugar; bring to the boil. Reduce heat and simmer for 5 minutes; adjust seasoning.

Pour soup into bowls and top with remaining bean shoots, tofu and shredded kaffir lime leaves. Garnish with coriander sprigs and serve immediately with a wedge of lime.

Substitute chicken with fish, prawns and even thin slices of pork fillet.
Any fresh or dried noodles can be used.
Tofu puffs are purchased from Asian grocers and some supermarkets.

warm haloumi salad

2 red capsicums
415g can chickpeas, drained and rinsed
2 chorizo sausages, thickly sliced
1 clove garlic, finely chopped
3 tablespoons extra virgin olive oil
zest and juice of one lemon
1 teaspoon sweet paprika
sea salt and freshly ground black pepper
250g haloumi cheese, cut into 16 pieces
100g baby spinach leaves

crusty bread to serve

Preheat a char-grill pan over high heat and cook whole capsicums for 10 minutes, turning frequently, until skins blister and blacken. Transfer to a large bowl and cover tightly with plastic wrap, or seal inside a plastic bag until cool. This will ensure that the skins slip off easily. Peel capsicums and slice flesh into long strips, discarding the seeds and membranes. Combine with chickpeas in a large serving bowl.

Cook sausage pieces 1-2 minutes or until crisp. Remove and add to the capsicums and chickpeas.

Mix together garlic, olive oil, lemon zest, juice and paprika in a small bowl; whisk to combine. Season with salt and pepper. Pour over the chickpea mixture.

Add a little extra oil and cook sliced haloumi for 30 seconds each side or until golden brown.

Add hot haloumi and spinach leaves to the chickpea mixture; toss well to combine. Serve with plenty of crusty bread

Capsicum can be cooked in a hot oven, 200°C/180°C (fan forced) for 20 minutes until skin blackens and blisters.
Substitute chorizo with your favourite spicy sausage.

japanese pancakes

serves 4

100g plain flour
1 teaspoon salt
2 eggs
½ cup water
150g white fleshed fish fillets, finely diced
1 cup shredded Chinese cabbage
4 green onions, chopped
2 tablespoons vegetable oil
Japanese mayonnaise, tonkatsu sauce and shredded nori, to serve

Place flour, salt, eggs and water into a large mixing bowl, and stir until well combined. Stir through fish, cabbage and green onions.

Heat one teaspoon of oil in a small non-stick frying pan over medium high heat.

Spoon a quarter of the pancake mixture into the frying pan. Spread mixture out to form a 15cm circle. Cook 2-3 minutes or until lightly browned.

Flip over pancake and cook the other side for a further 2 minutes. Repeat with remaining mixture.

To serve, drizzle with Japanese mayonnaise and tonkatsu sauce. Top with shredded nori. Serve immediately.

fresh
NINE NETWORK

For a variation, add ¼ cup of cooked corn to the pancake mixture.
Japanese mayonnaise and tonkatsu sauce are found in Asian stores.
Use any firm white fish such as Dory fillet.

spanish potato salad

1kg baby chat potatoes, halved

2 chorizo sausages, thinly sliced

400g can red kidney beans, rinsed and drained

1 red onion, thinly sliced

1 cup parsley leaves

dressing

1 tablespoon wholegrain mustard

1 tablespoon chopped fresh basil

2 tablespoons lemon juice

¼ cup olive oil

salt and pepper

Place potatoes in a large saucepan. Cover with cold water and bring to the boil. Cook for 10 minutes or until just tender. Drain immediately and refresh with cold water; set aside to cool.

Cook chorizo slices in a frying pan over medium heat for 2-3 minutes or until crispy and golden. Remove and drain on absorbent paper; cut slices in half.

Whisk dressing ingredients together and season with salt and pepper.

Combine potato, cooked chorizo, kidney beans, onion and parsley; drizzle over dressing and toss gently until just combined.

Serve immediately.

Substitute chorizo with any gourmet or spicy sausage.
For a vegetarian option, leave out the chorizo.

braised radicchio & gorgonzola gnocchi

2 tablespoons olive oil
1 garlic clove, chopped
100g pancetta, diced
200g radicchio, washed and thinly shredded
freshly ground black pepper, to taste
750g fresh gnocchi
50g gorgonzola cheese, crumbled

Heat oil in a large pan over medium heat. Add garlic and pancetta; cook, stirring frequently, for about five minutes or until pancetta is crispy.

Add radicchio and cook, stirring occasionally for 10 minutes or until radicchio has softened and collapsed. Season with pepper.

Bring a large saucepan filled with salted water to the boil. Add gnocchi and cook according to packet instructions. Drain, reserving a little of the cooking water. Transfer hot gnocchi and reserved water to pan with radicchio. Stir in half of the gorgonzola and mix well.

Spoon gnocchi into 4 serving plates. Crumble remaining gorgonzola evenly over the top of each.

Serve immediately.

If gorgonzola is too strong for the kids, replace with grated parmesan cheese.
Use any pasta instead of gnocchi if desired.

champagne & zucchini flower risotto

1.2 litres chicken stock
1 tablespoon olive oil
20g butter
2 medium onions, finely diced
1 clove garlic, crushed
2 cups carnaroli or arborio rice
1 cup Champagne or sparkling wine
salt and pepper

12 zucchini flowers, thinly sliced
⅔ cup crème fraiche
1 cup finely grated parmesan cheese
¼ small bunch chives, chopped
1 tablespoon shredded basil leaves
shaved parmesan, to serve

Place stock into a saucepan and bring to the boil; reduce heat and simmer gently.

Heat oil and butter together in a large saucepan; cook onions and garlic until softened and translucent. Add rice and cook, stirring for one minute to coat the rice in the buttery juices. Pour in Champagne and simmer 4-5 minutes or until liquid has almost evaporated.

Stirring continuously, add one ladleful of stock to rice and cook until almost absorbed. Continue in this manner until all but half a cup of stock remains; season with salt and pepper.

Add sliced zucchini flowers, remaining stock and crème fraiche; stir to combine and cook, covered for 5 minutes.

Just before serving, add shaved parmesan, chives and basil then mix well. Divide risotto into four large bowls and top with extra parmesan. Serve immediately.

fresh
9 NINE NETWORK

Use small, young zucchini if flowers aren't available.
A good quality stock improves the flavour of risottos.
Risottos are best served immediately.
Substitute the Champagne with your favourite white wine.

chicken, leek & tarragon pies

serves 4

2 tablespoons olive oil
2 leeks, thinly sliced
¼ cup plain flour
1½ cups hot chicken stock
2 cups cooked chicken meat, chopped
½ cup sour cream
2 tablespoons tarragon, chopped
salt and pepper

2 sheets puff pastry
½ cup cheddar cheese, grated
1 egg, beaten

Preheat oven to 220°C/200°C (fan forced).

Heat oil in a large saucepan over medium high heat and cook leeks for 2 minutes or until they soften and become translucent. Add flour and cook for 1 minute.

Gradually stir in stock and bring to the boil; reduce heat and cook for 5 minutes. Remove from heat and add cooked chicken, sour cream and tarragon; season with salt and pepper.

Place 1 sheet of pastry onto a lightly floured surface and sprinkle with cheese. Place second sheet of pastry on top and press down firmly. Using a 10cm wide ramekin as a guide, cut out four circles of pastry to form the lids.

Divide the filling between 4 ramekins and brush egg around the rims. Top with pastry circles and push down the edges onto the ramekins to seal.

Brush egg over the pastry and bake for 15 minutes or until pastry is crisp and golden.

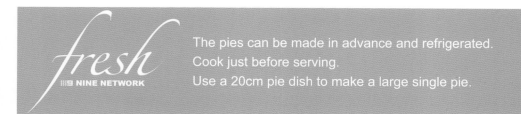

fresh
NINE NETWORK

The pies can be made in advance and refrigerated.
Cook just before serving.
Use a 20cm pie dish to make a large single pie.

chinese duck & roasted plum salad

serves 4

1 tablespoon brown sugar

1 tablespoon hoisin sauce

2 tablespoons peanut oil

1 Chinese barbecue duck, halved lengthways

3 ripe plums, quartered, stones removed

120g baby Asian greens

2 Lebanese cucumbers

4 green onions, thinly sliced

Preheat oven at 180°C/160°C (fan forced).

Combine brown sugar, hoisin and half of the oil in a small bowl, mix well and set aside.

Remove skin from duck breasts and slice into thin strips. Heat remaining oil in a large frying pan over medium high heat. Add skin and cook, stirring for about 2 minutes or until skin is crispy and golden. Drain on absorbent paper.

Remove duck meat from bones and slice thinly; put into a large baking dish. Brush hoisin sauce mixture over plums and place on top of duck meat. Cook for 15 minutes or until plums have softened slightly and duck meat is heated through.

Place salad leaves onto a platter or serving plates. Using a vegetable peeler, slice thin ribbons from cucumbers and arrange over salad leaves, scatter over green onions.

Gently toss through warm shredded duck, roasted plums with pan juices.

Scatter over crispy duck skin and serve immediately.

fresh
NINE NETWORK

Chinese barbecue duck is traditionally dipped and brushed during roasting with a sticky sweet coating made from soy sauce, sherry, ginger, five spice powder, star anise and hoisin sauce.

michelle's roast chicken

1.8 kg free range organic chicken (size 18)
2 lemons
4 whole cloves garlic
Pukara Estate garlic infused olive oil
sea salt and freshly ground black pepper

Preheat oven 200°C/180°C (fan forced).

Rinse chicken and pat dry with a paper towel; place into a baking dish, breast side up.

Cut one of the lemons into 4 wedges and place inside the cavity of the chicken with the cloves of garlic.

Squeeze the juice from the remaining lemon and brush over the skin of the chicken.

Generously pour garlic oil all over the skin and sprinkle with sea salt and freshly ground black pepper.

Roast 1½ hours, basting the chicken every 20 minutes with the pan juices. Remove chicken and rest, loosely covered with foil for 10 minutes before carving.

Serve with your favourite roasted vegetables.

fresh
NINE NETWORK

Add herbs such as rosemary, sage or tarragon.
Remember to collect the pan juices to make a delicious gravy.
Salt sprinkled over the skin makes it lovely and crispy.

roast duck in red curry

serves 4

400g can coconut cream

2 tablespoons red curry paste

2 cups chicken stock

3 baby eggplants, halved lengthways

200g pineapple, peeled, coarsely chopped

6 cherry tomatoes

2 kaffir lime leaves, torn

1 Chinese barbecue duck, chopped into large pieces

2 tablespoons fish sauce

2 tablespoons light soy sauce

1 tablespoon palm sugar, grated

1 long red chilli, sliced

¼ cup Thai basil leaves, torn

1 tablespoon lime juice

extra Thai basil leaves to garnish

steamed jasmine rice, to serve

Spoon ¼ cup of the coconut cream into a large wok. Cook over a medium high heat for 2 minutes, stirring continuously or until the coconut oil begins to separate from the cream (mixture will look like it has curdled.) Stir in curry paste and cook for a further 2 minutes or until fragrant. Stir in remaining coconut cream, stock and bring to the boil.

Add eggplants, pineapple, cherry tomatoes and kaffir lime leaves; simmer uncovered for about 2 minutes.

Add duck pieces, fish sauce, soy sauce and palm sugar; simmer for a further 10 minutes or until heated through. Remove from heat, stir in chilli, basil and lime juice.

Garnish with extra basil leaves. Serve hot with steamed jasmine rice.

Substitute duck with chicken, fish or beef.
Pineapple can be substituted with grapes or lychees.

beef dopiaza

2kg beef shin, boned

4 large brown onions, peeled

vegetable oil

1 cinnamon stick

1 teaspoon cardamom pods

½ teaspoon cloves

5 garlic cloves, crushed

6cm piece ginger, grated

2 teaspoons cumin seeds, crushed

1 tablespoon coriander seeds, crushed

1 teaspoon fenugreek seeds

½ teaspoon ground turmeric

½ cup plain yoghurt

2 cups water

2 long green chillies, chopped finely

1 teaspoon sea salt

½ teaspoon garam masala

Prepare beef by chopping into 4cm pieces, removing most of the fat or sinew.

Thinly slice 3 of the onions and cook in 2 tablespoons of oil until very tender and browned; remove from pan and set aside. Dice remaining onion; set aside.

Add beef in batches and cook until browned all over. Remove beef from pan and add to the cooked onions.

Add remaining oil and whole spices; cook for 30 seconds or until fragrant. To the same pan add the diced onion, garlic and ginger and cook until softened. Add crushed spices, fenugreek and turmeric and stir to combine.

Reduce heat to medium; add yoghurt a spoonful at a time, stirring to combine. Once all the yoghurt is added, return meat and onions to the pan with any juices, the water, chopped chillies and salt.

Stir to combine and bring to a gentle simmer. Partially cover and simmer 2 to 2½ hours until beef is tender.

Add garam masala. Check seasoning.

Serve with cardamom spiced rice or naan bread.

fresh
NINE NETWORK

Garam masala is a spice blend made up of coriander, cinnamon, cumin, nutmeg, cloves and cardamom.

Dopiaza means "onions twice". This could refer to the 2 methods of preparing the onions or the sheer quantity.

Either way it is a delicious winter warmer!

chilli, garlic & salt crusted beef fillet

serves 6-8

1 ½ teaspoons dried chilli flakes

2 cloves garlic

2 teaspoons sea salt

½ teaspoon black peppercorns

2 tablespoons olive oil

1kg beef eye fillet

oregano and rocket sauce

2 tablespoons fresh oregano leaves

1 clove garlic

zest and juice of a lemon

1 bunch rocket, chopped

½ slice of bread, crusts removed

salt and pepper to taste

½ cup olive oil

Combine chilli flakes, garlic, salt and peppercorns in a mortar and pestle. Pound until mixture is well combined, stir in oil. Rub mixture all over beef fillet and set aside. Preheat char-grill pan.

Cook beef fillet for 5 minutes on each side, or until cooked as desired. Transfer to a plate and cover with foil for 10 minutes to rest.

Meanwhile, blend or process oregano, garlic, lemon zest, half the lemon juice, bread, rocket and salt and pepper until coarsely chopped. Scrape down the sides of the processor and with the motor running, gradually add the olive oil. Taste the sauce and check the seasoning, you may or may not need any of the remaining lemon juice.

Slice beef fillet thinly and serve drizzled with oregano and rocket sauce.

If you don't have a mortar and pestle, use a small processor or spice grinder, or buy ground peppercorns and crush the garlic.

gnocchi topped cottage pie

750g potato gnocchi
½ cup grated tasty cheese

filling

2 tablespoons olive oil
1 brown onion, finely chopped
2 cloves garlic, crushed
2 zucchini, grated

2 carrots, grated
2 fresh bay leaves
1 kg beef mince
2 tablespoons plain flour
¼ cup tomato paste
2 tablespoons Worcestershire sauce
1 cup beef stock
salt and pepper, to taste

Preheat oven at 220°C/200°C (fan forced).

Cook gnocchi in a pot filled with plenty of boiling salted water. As soon as gnocchi has risen to the surface, drain, then rinse under cold water and toss in a little oil to prevent sticking.

To make filling; heat oil in a large frying pan. Add onion, garlic, zucchini, carrots and bay leaves. Cook, stirring for 2 minutes or until softened. Add mince, cook until browned all over. Stir in flour, tomato paste and Worcestershire sauce until well combined. Gradually stir in stock, bring to the boil; cook over a medium high heat, uncovered for 5 minutes or until thickened. Season with salt and pepper. Spoon into a shallow oven-proof dish. Top with gnocchi and cheese.

Cook for 25 minutes or until cheese has melted and mixture is bubbling.

fresh
NINE NETWORK

Traditionally, cottage pie is made with beef mince, topped with potato mash; substitute with lamb to make a Shepherd's pie.
Gnocchi made from potato is a great substitute for the mash.
This recipe also works well with chicken mince and chicken stock for a gnocchi topped chicken pie!

meatball sambo

serves 6

½ cup fresh breadcrumbs
½ cup cold milk
500g pork mince
500g veal mince
4 cloves garlic, crushed
½ cup finely grated parmesan cheese
1 teaspoon dried mixed herbs or 1 tablespoon chopped fresh herbs
2 eggs
salt and pepper

sauce

2 tablespoons olive oil
1 large brown onion, chopped finely
700ml bottle tomato passata
2 tablespoons tomato paste
1 sprig fresh basil

to serve

warm crusty white bread rolls, ciabatta or panini

Combine breadcrumbs and milk in a large mixing bowl. Add remaining ingredients and mix well with your hands, until the meat mixture sticks together. Shape into walnut sized balls and place on a tray.

Heat half the oil in a large non-stick frying pan and brown the meatballs in batches; transfer to a baking tray.

In the same frying pan, heat the remaining oil and cook the onion until it softens. Add tomato passata, tomato paste and basil and bring to a simmer. Stir in browned meatballs, simmer, uncovered for 10 minutes to cook the meatballs. Season to taste.

Remove from heat and allow the meatballs to sit in the sauce for 5 minutes to rest and allow the sauce to cool slightly.

To serve, butter warmed rolls and fill with meatballs and a little sauce. Serve with a crisp green salad.

fresh
NINE NETWORK

This is a great one to get the kids involved.

Meatball sandwiches are similar to the famous US sandwich 'Sloppy Joe' which is made with fried minced beef in a tomato sauce and served in a bun.

Meatballs are better if made the day before and gently reheated.

moroccan lamb with pumpkin couscous salad

serves 4

1½ cups natural yoghurt

1 tablespoon Moroccan spice mix

2 cloves garlic, crushed

salt and pepper, to taste

8 lamb fillets, trimmed

400g butternut pumpkin, peeled and cut into 2cm pieces

2 teaspoons olive oil

½ teaspoon chilli flakes

1½ cups hot chicken stock

1 cup couscous

½ cup flaked almonds, toasted

½ cup coriander leaves, plus extra for serving

¼ cup currants, soaked in boiling water for 5 minutes and then drained

Preheat oven at 180°C/160°C (fan forced).

Combine yoghurt, half of the spice mix, garlic, salt and pepper in a bowl. Toss lamb fillets in ½ cup of the yoghurt mixture; refrigerate the remaining yoghurt mixture for serving.

Toss together pumpkin, oil, remaining spice mix, chilli flakes and seasoning; place onto an oven tray lined with baking paper. Bake for 25 minutes, or until tender.

Pour hot stock over couscous in a medium bowl, cover and stand for 5 minutes. Toss through the roasted pumpkin, almonds, coriander and currants. Season with salt and pepper.

Grill lamb fillets on a hot preheated grill plate for approximately 2 minutes on each side or until cooked to your liking. Rest for 5 minutes before slicing diagonally.

To serve; divide couscous between 4 plates, top with lamb fillets, drizzle generously with reserved yoghurt mixture and finish with extra coriander leaves.

fresh
NINE NETWORK

Marinate the lamb fillets overnight for a more intense flavour.
Substitute pumpkin with kumara and almonds with pistachio.

lamb shank ragu

serves 6

2 tablespoons olive oil

3 medium lamb shanks

salt and pepper, to taste

2 cloves garlic

1 onion, diced

300ml red wine

2 medium carrots, finely chopped

4 cups chicken stock

400g can diced tomatoes

2 vine-ripened tomatoes, chopped

1 fresh bay leaf

500g fettucine pasta

grated parmesan cheese and crusty bread, to serve

Heat oil in a large pot or saucepan. Season the lamb shanks with salt and pepper. Cook shanks over a high heat until browned all over. Add garlic, onion and wine. Bring to the boil, simmer, uncovered for 5 minutes or until the wine has reduced by half.

Add carrots, stock, tomatoes and bay leaf, bring to the boil. Cover and simmer for 1½ hours or until the lamb is very tender and falls off the bone. Cool slightly and shred meat using tongs.

Cook pasta in plenty of boiling salted water until tender, drain, reserving a little of the cooking liquid. Transfer pasta and reserved liquid to a large bowl, toss with shredded lamb and cooking juices. Season with salt and pepper.

Serve with grated parmesan cheese and crusty bread.

fresh
NINE NETWORK

Use any long pasta you have in the cupboard.

This recipe also works well using gravy beef or lamb neck.

The term 'ragu' refers to a stew or a sauce for pasta (or any other starchy foods.)

lemongrass & pork stir fry

serves 4

2 stalks lemongrass, trimmed and finely chopped

2 cloves garlic, chopped

2 teaspoons white peppercorns

1 teaspoon sugar

2 tablespoons oil

400g pork fillet, trimmed and thinly sliced

500g fresh rice noodles

150g green beans, tailed and halved

2 tablespoons fish sauce

1 tablespoon kecap manis

Pound the lemongrass, garlic and peppercorns in a mortar and pestle until it forms a paste. Stir in sugar and 1 tablespoon of oil and stir through pork strips. Set aside to marinate for as long as possible.

Put noodles into a bowl and pour over boiling water. Stand for 2-3 minutes; drain and set aside.

Heat remaining oil in a wok over high heat. Add pork in small batches and stir fry for 1-2 minutes each or until sealed.

Return all pork to wok and add beans. Stir fry a further 2 minutes. Pour in fish sauce and kecap manis mix well.

Stir in noodles and toss until evenly coated and heated through. Serve immediately.

For successful stir frying, your wok must be hot. Add oil just before cooking. Slice meat thinly and cook in small batches to prevent wok from dropping in temperature and causing the meat to stew . Bring wok back up to heat between each batch.

Substitute pork with chicken, beef, prawns or a firm fish such as ling.

fennel roasted pork rack

⅓ cup fennel seeds
2 cloves garlic
1 tablespoon sea salt
2 tablespoons olive oil
1 x 12 rib, pork rack, frenched

1 tablespoon white vinegar
1 tablespoon olive oil, extra
2-3 teaspoons sea salt, extra

Preheat oven to 240°C/220°C (fan forced).

Combine fennel seeds, garlic, sea salt and olive oil in a mortar and pestle. Pound to a coarse paste.

Using a sharp knife, score the pork rind on the diagonal at 1cm intervals. Repeat scoring on the other diagonal to form a diamond pattern.

Brush pork rind with vinegar and extra olive oil; rub salt and fennel paste into the skin.

Line a large baking tray with baking paper, place seasoned pork on tray and place in the oven.

Bake for 20 minutes to form crackling. Reduce temperature to 180°C/160°C (fan forced) and bake for a further 30 minutes.

Drop temperature to 90°C/70°C (fan forced) and leave pork to rest in the oven for 20 minutes, or until ready to serve.

Carve pork, running knife between ribs to separate and serve with your favourite apple sauce.

fresh
NINE NETWORK

For a quick and delicious alternative, brush fennel paste over pork fillets and barbecue.
Salt and vinegar are the key to crisp crackling.
'Frenched' refers to meat trimmed to expose the bone. Ask your butcher to do this for you.

seafood stew

serves 4

1 tablespoon olive oil

1 medium brown onion, thinly sliced

2 cloves garlic, crushed

large pinch saffron

1 teaspoon of chilli flakes

1 cup white wine

2 tablespoons tomato paste

400g can crushed tomatoes

1½ cups fish stock

400g firm white fish, cut into 3cm pieces

12 mussels, cleaned and debearded

500g medium king prawns, shelled and deveined (tails intact)

2 tablespoons chopped parsley

salt and pepper

garlic and herb croutons

100g butter, softened

2 cloves garlic, crushed

1 teaspoon sea salt

1 tablespoon finely chopped basil

2 tablespoons finely grated parmesan

1 medium baguette, thickly sliced

Heat the oil in a large pan over medium heat, add onion and cook for 2-3 minutes or until softened. Add garlic, saffron, chilli and wine; simmer for 5 minutes. Stir in tomato paste, tomatoes and stock. Cook partially covered for 20-25 minutes or until sauce has thickened.

Combine butter, garlic, salt, basil and parmesan in a small bowl and mix well. Preheat grill on high and toast bread on one side. Remove and spread butter mixture thickly over other side of each slice. Return to grill, butter side up, and cook a further 1-2 minutes or until lightly golden.

Add fish, mussels and prawns to tomato mixture; cover and cook for a further 5 minutes or until mussels have opened. Stir in chopped parsley, season and serve with sliced baguette.

fresh
NINE NETWORK

Fresh mussels should smell like the sea. Only use ones that are closed, then open during cooking.

Use any fresh seafood that is in season, such as octopus, cuttlefish, pippis, clams or even green bugs.

barbecued cuttlefish, haloumi & lemon lentil salad

serves 4

¼ cup lemon juice

¼ cup extra virgin olive oil

extra olive oil, for brushing

salt and pepper, to taste

1 kg cuttlefish, cleaned and cut into thick strips

250g vine-ripened truss baby roma tomatoes

400g can lentils, rinsed and drained

100g baby rocket leaves

1 small red onion, thinly sliced

250g haloumi, sliced

Whisk together lemon juice, oil, season with salt and pepper. Pour half the dressing over cuttlefish strips and marinate for 10 minutes.

Heat a barbecue plate or char-grill pan over medium high heat. Brush tomatoes with a little oil; season with salt and pepper. Cook on grill for about 2 minutes or until just blistered and starting to soften; remove and set aside.

Drain cuttlefish from marinade and grill for 30 seconds on each side or until golden brown. Place hot cuttlefish into a large bowl with remaining dressing.

Brush haloumi with a little oil and grill for 30 seconds each side.

Combine lentils, rocket and onion with warm cuttlefish and dressing. Slice haloumi and mix through.

Serve immediately, topped with tomatoes.

fresh
NINE NETWORK

Cuttlefish, squid and octopus are interchangeable, so use whatever is available.

seafood lasagne

750g smoked haddock

5 cups milk

2 small bay leaves

½ teaspoon ground nutmeg

1 teaspoon black peppercorns

2 medium leeks, green parts reserved and white parts thinly sliced

200g butter

1 bulb fennel, trimmed and finely chopped

2 cloves garlic, crushed

⅔ cup plain flour

pinch cayenne pepper

2 tablespoon finely chopped dill

sea salt and freshly ground white pepper

1 kg medium green prawns, peeled with tails removed and lightly blanched in salted boiling water

3 medium zucchini, cut into ribbons with a vegetable peeler

700g tomato passata

8 fresh lasagne sheets

1 cup coarsely grated fontina cheese

½ cup finely grated parmesan

Preheat oven to 180°C/160°C (fan forced).

Combine haddock, milk, spices, bay leaves and green part of the leeks in a saucepan; bring to the boil. Reduce heat, cover and simmer 10 minutes. Drain, reserving milk. Flake haddock, removing bones, skin and spices

Melt butter in a pan and cook sliced leeks, fennel and garlic until soften. Stir in flour and cook a further 5 minutes. Gradually add reserved milk. Cook, stirring constantly, until sauce thickens. Remove from heat and add cayenne pepper, dill and flaked haddock; season to taste.

To make lasagne; pour a third of the passata into the base of a large 35cm x 28cm baking dish. Cover with two sheets of lasagne and top with a quarter of the haddock mixture. Layer over a quarter of the prawns and zucchini. Top with another third of the passata and two more sheets of pasta. Repeat layers, finishing with the lasagne sheets. Top with remaining haddock mixture and prawns. Sprinkle over combined cheeses and bake 40-50 minutes. Serve with crusty bread and mixed leaf salad.

This recipe is time consuming but well worth it!

If fresh lasagne is not available, substitute with dried lasagne sheets but increase cooking time by approximately 15 minutes.

garfish with zucchini & tomato crush

serves 4

¼ cup plain flour
2 tablespoons grated parmesan, (optional)
salt and pepper
8 garfish, scaled and gutted, heads removed

2 tablespoons olive oil
40g butter
2 cloves garlic, sliced thinly

3 medium zucchini, cut into 1cm pieces
250g punnet cherry tomatoes, halved
½ cup basil leaves, shredded
juice of half a lemon
salt and pepper

lemon wedges, to serve

Combine flour (parmesan if using) and seasoning on a large flat plate. Press garfish into flour to coat on both sides.

Heat half the oil and butter in a large frying pan. Add garlic and zucchini and cook for 4-5 minutes or until zucchini softens. Increase heat and add tomatoes, crushing lightly with a potato masher to release the juices. When vegetables are tender, remove from heat and stir in basil, lemon juice, salt and pepper to taste.

Heat remaining oil and butter in a second frying pan and cook garfish 1-2 minutes each side or until cooked as desired.

Serve garfish with zucchini and tomato mixture with extra lemon wedges on the side.

fresh
NINE NETWORK

Substitute garfish with sardines or small whole whiting if desired.
The tomato and zucchini crush goes well with steak and chicken.

wasabi pea crusted salmon

serves 4

1 cup packaged dried wasabi peas

4 x 180g salmon fillets, skinned and pin-boned

¼ cup Pukara wasabi infused olive oil

salt and pepper, to taste

1½ cups chicken stock

1 tablespoon lime juice

4 baby bok choy, quartered

Place wasabi peas in a mortar and pestle and crush until mixture resembles coarse breadcrumbs. Alternately pulse in a food processor. Transfer to a large flat plate.

Brush salmon fillets all over with a little oil and season with salt and pepper. Press one side of fillets into wasabi peas to form a crust.

Heat remaining oil in a large frying pan over medium high heat. Cook salmon, crust side down, for 2 minutes or until golden brown. Gently turn salmon fillets over and cook for a further 2 minutes or until cooked as desired. Remove and cover to keep warm.

Pour stock into same pan and stir to loosen pan scrapings, bring to the boil and simmer, uncovered for 5 minutes

Stir in lime juice, add bok choy, simmer for 2 minutes or until bok choy is just tender.

To serve, divide bok choy amongst four dinner bowls. Ladle stock evenly between bowls and top with salmon.

Wasabi peas are available at supermarkets and Asian stores.
Wasabi comes from the same family as cabbage, horseradish and mustard—it is known as Japanese horseradish.

chilli crumbed whiting with mushy peas

serves 4

1½ cups fresh breadcrumbs
1 teaspoon dried chilli flakes
1 teaspoon sweet paprika
2 teaspoons sea salt flakes
600g small whiting fillets
plain flour, for dusting
2 eggs, lightly beaten
sunflower oil, for shallow frying
lemon wedges and mint leaves, to garnish

mushy peas
4 cups frozen peas
½ cup chopped mint leaves
2 tablespoons olive oil
salt and pepper, to taste

To make mushy peas, place peas into a large heat-proof bowl. Pour over enough boiling water to cover; stand for 5 minutes. Drain and rinse under cold water, drain again. Using a stick blender, blend peas with mint and olive oil until thick. Season with salt and pepper.

Combine breadcrumbs, chilli, paprika, sea salt and mix until well combined.

Lightly dust fillets in flour, shaking off excess and then dip into beaten eggs. Place fillets into chilli breadcrumbs and push down on both sides to coat.

Heat enough oil in a large frying pan for shallow frying. Cook fish in batches until golden brown. Drain on paper towel.

Serve fish with mushy peas and garnish with lemon wedges and mint.

Use any firm white fish fillets such as flathead in this recipe.

home-made baked beans

serves 6

500g dried haricot beans

1 teaspoon bicarb soda

2 tablespoons olive oil

1 large onion, diced

3 cloves garlic, chopped

700g bottle passata

¼ cup treacle

¼ cup brown sugar

2 tablespoons Worcestershire sauce

1 tablespoon apple cider vinegar

2 bay leaves

1 tablespoon dried English mustard

¼ teaspoon ground cloves

¼ teaspoon smoked paprika

sea salt and freshly ground black pepper

2 cups chicken stock

1 small ham hock

In a medium saucepan combine beans and bicarb soda; cover with water. Bring to the boil, remove from heat immediately and allow to stand in the liquid for at least two hours. Return saucepan to the heat, bring to the boil again and drain.

Preheat oven to 160°C/140°C (fan forced).

Heat oil in a large enamelled cast-iron casserole dish; cook onion and garlic for 2-3 minutes or until softened.

Add the remaining ingredients, including the beans and bring to the boil. Place the ham hock on top of the beans; cover and place casserole in preheated oven for 4-5 hours.

Remove hock, discard skin and bone and shred meat. Return meat to beans and serve hot or cold on toast.

fresh
9 NINE NETWORK

Legumes are a family of more than 18,000 members. Not all of them are edible but those that are, we call pulses. The flavours improve with sitting. Store baked beans in a sealed container in the refrigerator for up to a week.

gozleme

200g plain yoghurt

pinch salt

250g self-raising flour, plus extra

100g baby spinach

200g feta cheese, crumbled

salt and pepper

2 tablespoons olive oil

50g butter, melted (optional)

lemon wedges to serve

Mix yoghurt and salt together in large bowl. Gradually add flour until you have a stiff dough. Tip onto a lightly floured surface and gradually knead dough, incorporating any remaining flour until the dough is soft and slightly sticky. Transfer to a clean bowl and stand, covered for 30 minutes.

On a floured surface, split the dough into 4 equal round pieces. Roll each piece of dough into a 30cm circle.

Place a quarter of the spinach over half a circle then sprinkle a quarter of the feta on top and season. Fold dough over and seal edges with a fork. Repeat this process with remaining dough, spinach and feta.

Preheat barbecue hot plate or large frying pan. Brush one side of each gozleme with olive oil and cook 1 to 2 minutes or until golden. Brush other side with olive oil, and cook for a further 2 minutes.

Brush with melted butter; cut into 4 and serve with lemon wedges.

Gözleme is a savoury pastry, enjoyed in Turkey as a meal or snack. Traditional versions include fried lamb mince or mashed potato. You can make the dough in advance as it will keep in the fridge for a few days.

lentil, cauliflower & egg curry

serves 4

2 tablespoons ghee or oil
2 onions, finely chopped
½ small cauliflower, cut into florets
3 cm piece ginger, finely grated
2 garlic cloves, crushed
2 tablespoons curry powder
2 teaspoons brown mustard seeds
5 curry leaves
1 teaspoon sugar

400g can chopped tomatoes
2 cups water or vegetable stock
400g can lentils, rinsed, drained
salt to taste
2 cups baby spinach leaves
4 hard-boiled eggs
½ cup coriander sprigs
wedges of lemon or lime

Heat ghee or oil in a large saucepan and cook onions, cauliflower, ginger and garlic until lightly browned and softened. Add spices, curry leaves and sugar; cook for 30 seconds.

Add tomatoes and water or stock and bring to the boil; add lentils and simmer 10 minutes or until curry thickens and reduces by a third.

Season to taste with salt and stir in the spinach leaves until wilted.

Divide the curry amongst serving bowls; top with halved eggs and coriander sprigs. Serve with lemon or lime wedges and basmati rice.

Substitute cauliflower with eggplant or broccoli.
If fresh curry leaves are not available, use dried ones but halve the quantity.

shakshuka eggs

2 green banana chillies

4 large vine-ripened tomatoes, diced

3 garlic cloves, finely chopped

2 teaspoons sweet paprika

⅓ cup olive oil

4 eggs

salt and pepper to taste

300g haloumi, cut into 4 slices

toasted sour dough to serve

Cook banana chillies over a high heat on a grill or barbecue plate until blackened and blistered. Place into a plastic bag until cool. This will allow the skins to be removed easily. Peel off blackened skins and scrape out seeds and membrane. Cut flesh into 1cm thick strips and set aside.

Place tomatoes, garlic, paprika and a quarter cup of olive oil in a large frying pan. Simmer, covered over a medium heat for 10 minutes or until tomatoes have collapsed; stir in chilli. Simmer, uncovered for a further 8-10 minutes or until all the juices have evaporated and the sauce has thickened.

Using a wooden spoon push the sauce to the side of the pan, allowing space for the eggs. Break eggs into pan and then season; cover and cook for about 2 minutes or until the eggs are cooked to your liking.

Heat a char-grill pan over medium heat. Brush haloumi and bread with remaining oil and cook on both sides until golden brown.

Serve toasted bread with shakshuka sauce, eggs and haloumi.

This recipe is inspired by the traditional Israeli version.
It is a great brunch idea—you could add bacon or grilled prosciutto.

tamari snacks

100g packet plain rice crackers
1 cup whole almonds
1 cup cashew nuts
½ cup pepitas
½ cup sunflower seeds
⅓ cup tamari soy sauce

Preheat oven 160°C/140°C (fan forced).

Combine crackers, almonds, cashews, pepitas and sunflower seeds in a large bowl. Pour over tamari, toss well until evenly coated. Stand at room temperature for 10 minutes.

Place on two large baking trays lined with baking paper; bake 25-30 minutes until nuts are dry roasted, cool. Store in an airtight container.

Whole nuts have far lower GI than chopped ones. Anything that needs to be chewed and processed by the body has a lower GI.
Tamari is a dark, thick sauce made from soybeans. It is similar in flavour to soy sauce.

tomato kasundi

8cm fresh ginger, peeled
10 cloves garlic, peeled
2 long green chillies, split and seeded
1 large onion, peeled and roughly chopped
½ cup vegetable oil
1 tablespoon black mustard seeds
2 curry leaves
1 tablespoon turmeric
2 tablespoons ground cumin
1 tablespoon paprika
1 tablespoon dry mustard
½ cup brown malt vinegar
1.5 kg roma tomatoes, washed and roughly chopped
1 cup sugar
1½ tablespoons salt

Combine the ginger, garlic, chillies and onion in a blender and process until smooth.

Heat half the oil in a large pan over medium heat. Add mustard seeds and fry until they 'pop'.

Add curry leaves, spices, and the garlic and chilli paste; cook another minute or until fragrant.

Add the remaining ingredients and bring to the boil. Reduce heat; simmer, stirring occasionally for 1 hour or until thick and 'jammy'.

Spoon into sterilised jars. Cap and store in the refrigerator.

Kasundi is like a relish—use it on sandwiches or serve with steak or chicken.
Keep refrigerated for a week.
For a spicier version, substitute the paprika with 1 teaspoon of chilli powder.

chocolate hazelnut stack

serves 8

½ cup hazelnuts, toasted
6 egg whites
1⅔ cups caster sugar
1½ teaspoons white vinegar
¼ cup cocoa powder
600ml thickened cream
2 punnets fresh raspberries

Preheat oven 150°C/130°C (fan forced).

Process hazelnuts until they resemble fine breadcrumbs; set aside.

In a large bowl beat egg whites until stiff peaks form. Add sugar a little at a time, beating until sugar dissolves with each addition; add vinegar with the last of the sugar and beat to combine.

Carefully fold through 2 tablespoons of cocoa powder and three quarters of the hazelnuts into the meringue.

Using a 22cm round cake tin or plate as a guide, trace 3 circles on sheets of baking paper.

Grease 3 flat baking trays and place baking paper, drawn side down, onto trays. Divide the meringue mixture into 3 and spread onto each baking sheet using the drawn circle as a guide. Sprinkle remaining cocoa and hazelnuts over one of the meringues.

Bake 55-60 minutes or until meringue feels dry to the touch and lifts easily off the baking paper; cool completely in oven.

Whip cream until thick and set aside.

Keep the cocoa and nut-dusted meringue for the top. Spread half the cream over one of the other meringues and top with half the raspberries; place remaining meringue on top, spread with more cream and raspberries. Finally top with reserved cocoa and nut meringue.

Cut into thick wedges and serve immediately.

fresh
NINE NETWORK

Assemble meringue stack at the last minute or the cream will soften the meringue and may cause the stack to collapse.
Cool meringue in oven with door slightly ajar to prevent meringue from cracking.

margherita sorbet

2 cups water

1½ cups sugar

¾ cup fresh lime juice

1 tablespoon finely grated lime rind

¼ cup Tequila

¼ cup Triple Sec or Cointreau

2 egg whites

Murray River sea salt flakes, to serve

lime slices and grated lime rind, to serve

Place water and sugar in a medium saucepan; stir over a low heat until sugar dissolves. Bring to the boil; boil uncovered for 2 minutes. Remove from heat and cool completely. Stir in lime juice, rind, alcohol and 1 egg white. Refrigerate until cold. Pour mixture into an ice cream maker and freeze according to manufacturer's instructions.

Alternatively, spoon mixture into a food storage container and freeze until solid. Transfer mixture to a food processor and process until smooth; refreeze.

To serve, dip the rims of four margherita glasses into remaining egg white and then into sea salt and spoon frozen margherita mixture evenly amongst glasses.

Use any alcohol you desire; Vodka, Gin or Grand Marnier works well.
Murray River sea salt is pink which adds a tinge of colour to the rim.

turkish delight cake

250g unsalted butter, room temperature
1 cup caster sugar
zest of 2 lemons, finely grated
4 eggs
½ cup Greek style yoghurt
¼ cup lemon juice
1 teaspoon rosewater
250g fine semolina
125g almond meal
¾ cup self-raising flour, sifted
double cream and icing sugar, to serve

syrup
1½ cups caster sugar
¼ cup honey
1 cup water
¼ cup orange juice
1 teaspoon rosewater
1 cassia stick
4 cardamom pods, bruised
½ cup dried rose buds
¼ cup pistachio kernels, coarsely chopped
½ cup diced Turkish Delight

Preheat oven to 180°C/160°C (fan-forced). Grease a 20cm square cake pan, line base and sides with baking paper.

Beat butter, sugar in large bowl with an electric mixer until pale and creamy. Add zest. Gradually add eggs, one at a time, beating until well combined.

Add yoghurt, lemon juice, rosewater, then combined semolina, almond meal and flour; gently fold until just combined. Spoon into prepared pan, smooth over top.

Bake for 50-55 minutes or until top is golden brown and a skewer comes out clean when inserted into centre of cake.

To make syrup, place all ingredients except the pistachios and Turkish Delight in a medium saucepan. Stir over a low heat until sugar dissolves. Bring to the boil, remove from heat and refrigerate until cool. Once cold, stir in pistachios and Turkish Delight.

Remove cake from oven and allow to cool slightly in pan. Turn out onto a serving plate and spoon over syrup.

Serve warm or cool with cream; dust with icing sugar.

fresh
NINE NETWORK

This cake is very exotic and is perfect for any dinner party, baby shower or romantic dinner.

anise chocolate log with chilli caramel sauce

serves 8-10

2 star anise
300ml thickened cream
500g dark chocolate, chopped
2 tablespoons glucose syrup

chilli caramel sauce
1 long red chilli
¾ cup brown sugar
½ cup pouring cream
100g cold salted butter, chopped
Persian fairy floss and vanilla ice cream, to serve

Grease a 6 cup capacity bar pan or terrine mould. Line base and sides with baking paper, extending 5 cm above pan edges.

Place star anise and cream into a medium saucepan; bring to the boil. Remove from heat, add chocolate to saucepan. Return pan to heat, stir continuously over a low heat until mixture is smooth; stir in glucose. Remove anise and pour mixture into prepared pan. Cover and refrigerate overnight or until firm.

To make chilli caramel, place chilli in a medium bowl. Pour boiling water over chilli to cover and stand for 5 minutes, drain. Cut chilli in half lengthways, remove and discard seeds and membrane. Place sugar, cream and butter in a medium saucepan, stir continuously over a low heat until butter has melted. Bring to boil, add chilli, remove from heat and stand for 10 minutes to cool slightly and for chilli to infuse.

Turn anise chocolate log out onto a serving plate and pour over warm chilli caramel. Top with fairy floss and serve with ice cream.

fresh
::9 NINE NETWORK

Pouring the water over the chilli is a Vietnamese practice. It takes out some of the heat from the chilli but leaves behind the natural perfume and taste. This technique is perfect for a dessert.

brownie affogato

250g unsalted butter, melted

400g dark chocolate, chopped

½ cup brown sugar

½ cup caster sugar

4 eggs

2½ cups plain flour

250g block Caramello chocolate, chopped

extra 200g dark chocolate, chopped

raspberries, to serve

vanilla ice cream

espresso coffee

Preheat oven 180°C/160°C (fan forced). Grease a 19 x 30cm lamington pan. Line base and sides with baking paper, extending about 2cm above pan edges.

Place butter and dark chocolate in a large saucepan. Stir over a low heat until chocolate has melted. Remove from heat, stir in sugars. Cool at room temperature for 10 minutes.

Gradually beat in eggs using a wooden spoon or spatula. Stir in flour until well combined and then Caramello and extra chocolate. Spoon mixture into prepared pan, smooth over top.

Bake for 30 minutes, remove from oven (top of brownie should feel a little soft to touch and inside should still be moist).

To serve, place a triangle piece of brownie into a martini glass or serving dish with some fresh raspberries. Top with a scoop of vanilla ice cream and pour over a shot of espresso coffee.

fresh ⠿⠿ NINE NETWORK

Make a large batch of brownies and it will freeze well. Wrap tightly in foil or cling film and freeze for up to 2 months.

Fold brownie pieces through softened ice cream to make a 'cookies and cream' style ice cream - a great way to make your own indulgent ice cream without buying the expensive ones.

traditional trifle

madeira cake

170g butter, softened
170g caster sugar
4 eggs
250g self raising flour, sifted
½ cup milk
zest of 1 lemon

custard

⅓ cup caster sugar
1½ tablespoons cornflour
6 egg yolks
1½ cups milk
1½ cups cream
1 teaspoon vanilla extract

1 cup raspberries, fresh or frozen
⅔ cup raspberry jam, warmed
½ cup sweet sherry
600ml thickened cream, whipped
1 cup flaked almonds, toasted

Preheat oven at 180°C/160°C (fan forced).

Grease a 2 litre (8 cup) capacity loaf tin. Line base and sides with baking paper.

Beat butter and sugar together in a medium bowl with an electric beater until pale and fluffy. Add eggs one at a time beating until well combined. Gently fold in flour, milk and zest until well combined. Spoon the mixture into the loaf tin and smooth over top.

Cook 35–40 minutes or until a skewer when inserted comes out clean. Remove from the oven and cool in the tin for 10 minutes, turn out onto a wire rack to cool.

To make custard; whisk sugar and cornflour in a large bowl. Whisk in egg yolks, cream, milk and vanilla until smooth. Transfer to a saucepan and cook over medium heat, stirring constantly until mixture just comes to the boil. Remove from heat and refrigerate until cold.

Cut cake in half lengthways and then into 1cm slices. Place a third of the raspberries into the bottom of a large serving bowl, arrange half the cake over the top. Spoon over half the raspberry jam and another third of the raspberries. Top with remaining cake, spread with remaining raspberry jam and raspberries. Pour sherry over cake and allow to soak. Top with custard. Cover and refrigerate for at least 2 hours until custard is set.

Spoon whipped cream over trifle and sprinkle with toasted almonds.

fresh
NINE NETWORK

This is traditional English trifle that does not include jelly and is best made the day before.
For a quick trifle, use a store-bought sponge or madeira cake.
Keep on eye on the custard. If allowed to boil, it will curdle.

roasted winter fruit salad

2 plums, halved

2 buerre bosc pears, cored, quartered

125g punnet raspberries

2 green apples, peeled, quartered

1 cup fresh dates

½ cup dried raisins

1 cup red grapes

1 vanilla bean, halved and scraped

1 cinnamon stick

⅓ cup brown sugar

50g unsalted butter, melted

cinnamon ice cream

8 egg yolks

½ cup caster sugar

2 cups milk

2 cups cream

1 teaspoon ground cinnamon

½ x 250g packet butternut biscuits, crushed

½ cup chopped pecans

To make ice cream; whisk yolks and sugar together in a bowl. Place milk, half the cream and cinnamon into a large saucepan and bring to the boil. Whisk a quarter of the hot milk mixture into yolk mixture and mix well. Pour yolk mixture back into the saucepan with remaining hot milk.

Cook over a medium low heat, stirring continuously with a spatula or flat bottomed wooden spoon until mixture thickens and just coats the back of a spoon. Stir in remaining cream and pour into a bowl; cover and refrigerate until cold.

Churn custard in ice cream maker according to manufacturer's instructions. Alternatively pour into a deep baking dish, and freeze for one hour. Run a whisk through mixture every 30 minutes until firm. Add biscuits and nuts halfway during churning. Freeze for several hours or until firm.

Preheat oven at 220°C/200°C (fan forced)

Place fruit, vanilla, cinnamon with sugar and butter into a large baking dish. Bake 25 minutes or until just tender.

Serve warm fruit topped with ice cream scoops.

fresh NINE NETWORK

A cheat's version; stir biscuits and pecans through softened, bought vanilla ice cream and refreeze.
Use any type of biscuit you wish in the ice cream and any fruit in season.
The raspberries will break down whilst cooking to help make a nice jammy sauce for the other fruit.
If raspberries are not in season, use frozen berries or ½ cup of your favourite jam.

We really hope you enjoyed these recipes and may they bring you many hours of cooking joy!

Here's how to keep up to date with the latest Fresh recipes:

Watch **Fresh** Monday to Friday on the Nine Network.
check local guides

Visit our website www.ninemsn.com.au/fresh

Download our free "What's for dinner?" podcasts,
see our website for more details

Enjoy
the Fresh team